Spotlight on™ Reading & Listening
Figurative Lan

by Paul F. Johnson & Carolyn LoGiudice

Skills	Ages
■ reading	■ 11 and up
■ listening	**Grades**
	■ 6 and up

Evidence-Based Practice

■ Explicitly teaching and reinforcing inference-making leads to better outcomes in overall text comprehension, text engagement, and metacognitive thinking (Borné, Cox, Hartgering, & Pratt, 2005).

■ Summarization is a skill that helps students identify main ideas, generalize what they've read, and recall information needed to answer comprehension questions (NRP, 2000).

■ Instruction in comprehension can help students understand, remember, and communicate with others about what they read (NIFL, 2003).

■ Teacher questioning improves students' learning from reading because it gives them a purpose for reading, focuses their attention on what they are to learn, helps them think actively as they read, encourages them to monitor their comprehension, and helps them review content and relate what they've learned to what they already know (NIFL, 2003).

■ Effective listening strategies include (NCLRC, 2004):
  • Listening for details and main ideas
  • Predicting
  • Drawing inferences
  • Summarizing
  • Recognizing word-order patterns

Spotlight on Reading & Listening Comprehension Level 2 incorporates these principles and is also based on expert professional practice.

References

Borné, L., Cox, J., Hartgering, M., & Pratt, E. (2005). *Making inferences from text* [Overview]. Dorchester, MA: Project for School Innovation.

National Capital Language Resource Center (NCLRC). (2004). *Strategies for developing listening skills.* Retrieved June 15, 2009, from www.nclrc.org/essentials/listening/stratlisten.htm

National Institute for Literacy (NIFL). (2003). *Put reading first: The research building blocks for teaching children to read.* Retrieved June 15, 2009, from www.nifl.gov/nifl/publications.html

National Reading Panel (NRP). (2000). *Teaching children to read: An evidence-based assessment of the scientific research literature on reading and its implications for reading instruction–Reports of the subgroups.* Retrieved June 15, 2009, from http://www.nichd.nih.gov/publications/nrp/upload/smallbook_pdf.pdf

LinguiSystems

LinguiSystems, Inc.
3100 4th Avenue
East Moline, IL 61244
800-776-4332

FAX: 800-577-4555
Email: service@linguisystems.com
Web: linguisystems.com

Printed in the U.S.A.
ISBN 978-0-7606-0733-6

About the Authors

Paul F. Johnson, B.A., and **Carolyn LoGiudice**, M.S., CCC-SLP, are editors and writers for LinguiSystems. They have collaborated to develop several publications, including *Story Comprehension To Go*, *No-Glamour Sequencing Cards*, and *Spotlight on Reasoning & Problem Solving*. Paul and Carolyn share a special interest in boosting students' language, critical thinking, and academic skills.

In their spare time, Paul and Carolyn enjoy their families, music, gourmet cooking, and reading. Paul, a proud father of three children, also enjoys bicycling, playing music, and spending rare moments alone with his wife, Kenya. Carolyn is learning to craft greeting cards and spoil grandchildren.

Cover design by Jeff Taylor

Editing and page layout by Karen Stontz

Table of Contents

Introduction

Spotlight on Reading & Listening Comprehension was developed in 2005 to provide controlled reading materials for improving both overall and specific comprehension skills. Six separate booklets presented passages with readabilities that varied from grades 2.0 through 4.9 along with follow-up comprehension questions. Each booklet focused on one of these key reading comprehension skills:

- Characters & Actions
- Comparing & Contrasting
- Figurative Language & Exclusion

- Making Inferences & Drawing Conclusions
- Paraphrasing & Summarizing
- Sequencing & Problem Solving

Requests for a similar approach to reading comprehension skill-building that would be more appealing to older students has resulted in *Spotlight on Reading & Listening Comprehension, Level 2*. Not only are the readabilities of the passages increased in this series, but the content and visual elements are designed to appeal to older students reading below grade level.

Each booklet includes stories and comprehension questions for detecting the main idea, identifying details, and thinking about the vocabulary and semantics in the passage. In addition, each booklet includes comprehension questions for a specific skill area. This particular booklet features questions that require students to understand figurative language in what they have read. The other five booklets focus on these skill areas:

- Comparing & Contrasting
- Understanding Everyday Information
- Fact & Opinion

- Paraphrasing & Summarizing
- Making Inferences & Drawing Conclusions

The readability of the passages Is controlled, based on the Flesch-Kincaid readability statistics. These statistics were revised in 2002; the new statistics yield a higher grade level in most cases than the previous ones. The range in readability is from grade levels 4.0 through 6.9. Each booklet includes eleven passages with the following readability ranges:

- Passages 1-3   Readability 4.0-4.9
- Passages 4-7   Readability 5.0-5.9
- Passages 8-11   Readability 6.0-6.9

The question pages for each passage also ask students to formulate questions about what they have read. The last task for each passage is a related writing prompt.

Use these passages for groups of students or individuals. Photocopy the material so each student has a copy. Encourage your students to highlight or underline key information as they read each passage and to jot down any questions they have.

Research proves that repeated readings improve reading comprehension and that three reads are usually sufficient repetition for a student to grasp the content, assuming a passage is at or below the student's reading competency level. We recommend training students to read a passage three times for adequate comprehension before trying to answer the comprehension questions.

The reading comprehension questions are similar to those found on classroom and national reading comprehension tests. Have your students read each possible answer for the multiple-choice questions before they select their answers.

As you present information to your students, model your own reading comprehension strategies. Talk about ways to rescan a passage to find key information and other tips that will help your students improve their reading competence and confidence.

We hope you will find *Spotlight on Reading & Listening Comprehension, Level 2* a welcome resource to help students understand and find satisfaction in what they read.

Paul and Carolyn

Story 1

For many months, Nelson prepared for the next annual spelling bee. He practically had a lock on the local contest again this year. The state competition, though, was a horse of a different color.

Nelson kept his nose to the grindstone all summer, turning deaf ears to his friends' invitations. Winning the state spelling bee meant the world to him.

As expected, Nelson won the local bee with flying colors. Today was the state contest. It was a red-letter day for Nelson. He had as many butterflies in his stomach as the other contestants, but he had a one-track mind. He focused on the task at hand and kept his nerves in check. He spelled his first word correctly, getting off to a solid start.

Each round was more difficult. At last only two spellers were left, Nelson and Anna. Anna's word was *cerebroside*. "C-E-R-E-B-R-O-C-Y-D-E," she spelled. She smiled, pleased as punch with her answer.

"That is incorrect," said the judge. "Nelson, would you please give it a shot?"

"C-E-R-E-B-R-O-S-I-D-E," he spelled.

"Congratulations, Nelson," said the judge. "You are our new state champion speller!" Nelson was thrilled to his core. He was on top of the world. Nothing could rain on his parade today, and no one could burst his bubble. Time to celebrate!

Main Idea and Details

1. What is the main idea of this story?

   a. Nelson became the state spelling champion.

   b. Nelson learned to spell tough words.

   c. Nelson wanted to celebrate.

2. What did Nelson hope to achieve?

   a. to win the local spelling championship

   b. to win the state spelling championship

   c. to win the national spelling championship

3. Why was winning the spelling bee so important to Nelson?

   a. He wanted the prize money.

   b. He wanted to impress people.

   c. The story doesn't say.

Vocabulary and Semantics

4. What does **annual** mean?

   a. important

   b. yearly

   c. renewal

5. What does it mean to **have a one-track mind**?

   a. to think about trains and transportation

   b. to be stubborn about getting your own way

   c. to think about just one thing

6. **Nelson focused on the task at hand**. What does that mean?

   a. He concentrated on the task.

   b. He agreed to do the task.

   c. He looked closely at his hand.

Figurative Language

7. Which expression doesn't mean the same thing as to **have a lock on something**?

    a. to have it in writing

    b. to be uptight about it

    c. to have it for sure

8. Which expression doesn't mean the same thing as **a horse of a different color**?

    a. a fly in the ointment

    b. an entirely different matter

    c. a different story

9. What does it mean to **turn deaf ears to something**?

    a. to find it hard to hear something

    b. to listen without saying anything

    c. to ignore something

10. What did the judge mean when he asked Nelson to **give it a shot**?

    a. to aim his weapon at the target

    b. to try it

    c. neither of the above

Asking Questions

Ask a question about selecting the words for a spelling bee.

Writing and Discussion Prompt ·······························

This story doesn't explain why winning the state championship was so important to Nelson. Suggest at least one logical reason the state championship meant the world to Nelson. Then explain what it would mean to you to be the champion speller for your state or province.

9

Story 2

Photo courtesy of istockphoto.com © Sharon Dominick

Math has always been difficult for Darcy. Last year she passed geometry by the skin of her teeth. She definitely has her work cut out for her this year. Her algebra class is already a nightmare. Darcy is oblivious how to keep her head above the water.

Unfortunately, Darcy has an algebra assignment due tomorrow that will count for 10% of her grade for the quarter. Sooner or later, she will have to get her act together and face the music.

With the enthusiasm of a dried fig, Darcy drags herself to her desk. She opens her algebra book and heaves a slow sigh. "This is ridiculous!" she thinks. "Algebra will be the death of me. Where is the light at the end of this tunnel?"

Darcy's big brother pops into her room. "Hey, Darcy, I hear you're taking algebra this year. That class was a snap for me. Let's get cracking on that homework. Two heads are better than one."

Darcy's face lights up. "You're on!" she exclaims.

Readability 4.3
Copyright © 2007 LinguiSystems, Inc.

Main Idea and Details

1. What is the main idea of this story?

    a. Darcy's brother is helpful.

    b. Darcy has a math assignment.

    c. Darcy needs her brother's help with algebra.

2. Why is it so important for Darcy to do well on her algebra assignment?

    a. It will count for 20% of her grade this quarter.

    b. It is worth 10% of her grade this quarter.

    c. It will count for 10% of her grade this semester.

3. Why does Darcy's brother think he can help her?

    a. He already knows what she needs to learn.

    b. He is older than she is.

    c. He is smarter than she is.

Vocabulary and Semantics

4. Which word is a synonym for **oblivious**?

    a. clueless

    b. lifeless

    c. careless

5. Which word means the same as **get cracking**?

    a. break

    b. start

    c. cheat

6. Which of these is not a meaning for **quarter**?

    a. a coin worth 25 cents

    b. half of a football game

    c. one-fourth of a school year

Figurative Language

7. Which expression means the opposite of **by the skin of her teeth**?

   a. by a mile

   b. by her toes

   c. by hook or by crook

8. Why did Darcy need to **keep her head above the water**?

   a. so she wouldn't sink

   b. so she could pass the class

   c. so she could get some help

9. Which expression doesn't mean the same as **face the music**?

   a. deal with it

   b. get on with it

   c. play with it

10. Why did Darcy want to **see the light at the end of the tunnel**?

    a. There wasn't enough light to do her homework.

    b. She was searching for hope.

    c. She wanted to take a trip to get away from algebra.

Asking Questions

Ask a question about facing the music when you have to meet a challenge.

Writing and Discussion Prompt ································

Darcy was lucky to have a brother who could come to her rescue. If he hadn't

been around, what else could Darcy have done to deal with her algebra troubles?

Story 3

Christina braced herself and tried to keep her cool while Dr. Culpepper prepared to fill a cavity. "All I have to do is sit tight and keep myself together. Now is not the time to freak out," she told herself.

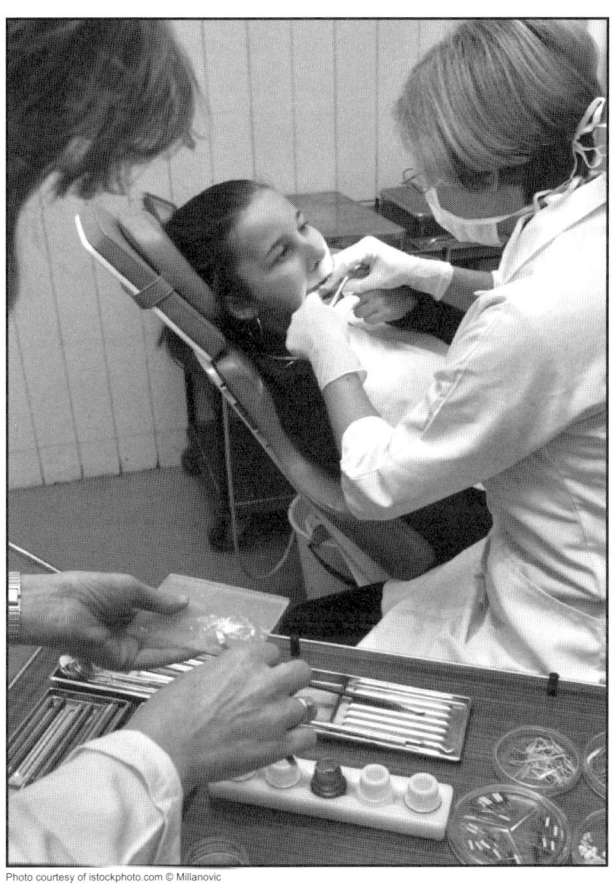

Photo courtesy of istockphoto.com © Millanovic

Christina was usually as calm as a cucumber, but there's something about being trapped in a dentist's chair while a dentist inserts tools into your mouth that puts even the bravest soul on edge. What if the dentist accidentally slips with the drill? What if the Novocain wears off before Dr. Culpepper is done with my tooth? These and other thoughts raced through Christina's head. Her hands were as cold as ice.

"I hear you're on the swim team this year, Christina. Congratulations!" said Dr. Culpepper. Christina couldn't possibly answer. She wondered why dentists even try to talk to their patients while they work on them. It's impossible to talk with your mouth full of cotton, tools, and fingers.

"Almost done, Christina," Dr. Culpepper reassured her. In the blink of an eye, Christina had her mouth back to herself. No more drilling or poking with metal instruments. Her mouth felt like a thick sock and her lips were numb. She was eager to go home. This was one day she would be glad to put behind her.

Main Idea and Details

1. What is the main idea of this story?

    a. Christina hopes to become a dentist.

    b. Christina's dentist fills a cavity for her.

    c. Novocain doesn't always last long enough.

2. What kind of team is Christina on this year?

    a. swimming

    b. bowling

    c. tennis

3. Where was Christina going after her dental appointment?

    a. to practice with her team

    b. to the library

    c. home

Vocabulary and Semantics

4. What does it mean to **brace yourself**?

    a. to hold onto your leg

    b. to put yourself into a brace so you won't move

    c. to prepare yourself to face something

5. Which word doesn't mean about the same as **being on edge**?

    a. amazed

    b. anxious

    c. nervous

    d. jumpy

6. **Dr. Culpepper prepared to fill a cavity**. What does that mean?

    a. She studied about how to fill a cavity.

    b. She got things ready to fill a cavity.

    c. She finished filling a cavity.

Figurative Language

7. Which expression doesn't belong in this group?

    a. Keep your cool.

    b. Sit tight.

    c. Freak out.

    d. Hold yourself together.

8. Which emotion doesn't go with **having hands as cold as ice**?

    a. fear

    b. joy

    c. anxiety

9. Which word means the same as **in the blink of an eye**?

    a. quickly

    b. clearly

    c. later

10. What does it mean to **put the day behind her**?

    a. to turn around and think about something else

    b. to be brave about something you fear during the day

    c. to reach the end of the day and forget what happened

Asking Questions

Ask a question about having a conversation with a dentist during a dental appointment.

Writing and Discussion Prompt ••••••••••••••••••••••••••••••••

Christina set herself a goal of staying in control of herself during her appointment. Write or talk about what you do when you want to have good self-control.

Story 4

Julio and Benjamin are longtime friends who reside in the same neighborhood. Ordinarily they communicate well. They talk straight and are there for each other like good friends. Sometimes, like today, there's a rip in the fabric of their friendship.

Julio was trying to impress his new girlfriend, Roxanne, who was hanging with her friends. Things were working fine until Benjamin appeared on the scene and joined the group. He imitated everything Julio said, adopting a fake accent and a falsetto voice. The girls thought it was funny, but Julio was less than thrilled. In fact, he was humiliated.

Julio pulled Benjamin aside and said, "I'd like to get something off my chest. I've got a bone to pick with you. You have no right to mock me or the way I talk, especially in front of anyone."

"Keep your shirt on, Julio," said Benjamin. "I was just messing with you. Don't be so sensitive! If you play your cards right, Roxanne will fall for you and you'll live happily ever after. Don't even give me a second thought. I'm just your old, discarded friend."

Main Idea and Details

1. What is the main idea of this story?

   a. Students make fun of each other.

   b. Good friends have a problem.

   c. Julio has a speech problem.

2. Who was talking to Roxanne and her friends first?

   a. Julio

   b. Benjamin

   c. neither of the above

3. What did Benjamin do that annoyed Julio?

   a. made fun of what he said

   b. flirted with Roxanne

   c. mocked the way Julio spoke

   d. both *a* and *c*

Vocabulary and Semantics

4. Which word is not a synonym for **reside**?

   a. dwell

   b. beside

   c. live

5. What is a **falsetto** voice?

   a. a high-pitched voice

   b. a rough, scratchy voice

   c. a low-pitched voice

6. True or false? When you are **humiliated**, you are embarrassed.

Figurative Language

7. What does it mean to **talk straight**?

    a. talk without stopping for a long time

    b. compliment someone

    c. tell the truth

    d. both *b* and *c*

8. What does it mean to **adopt** a fake accent?

    a. take on

    b. borrow

    c. try

9. What is another way to say **don't give me a second thought**?

    a. Ignore me.

    b. Don't tell me what to do again.

    c. Give me just your first thought.

10. What did Benjamin mean about being a **discarded friend**?

    a. He thought Julio hated him.

    b. He thought Julio thought he was disgusting.

    c. He thought Julio didn't want to be with him anymore.

Asking Questions

Ask a question about friendship.

Writing and Discussion Prompt ·······································

Write or talk about what probably happened between Julio and Benjamin before this story began. Explain why Benjamin and Julio might need to talk straight about what's going on between them.

Announcing

Ginanelli's Pizza!

Are you tired of bland, boring pizza?

Are you looking for *pizza with pizzazz?*

Look no further!

Ginanelli's incredible pizza will knock your socks off with your very first taste!

Our pizza is out of this world!
Our flavorful sauce packs a punch with its exotic combination of spices.
Made with love, our hand-tossed dough yields the lightest, crispiest,
crunchiest crust you've ever known.
Once you try our pizza, you'll quit eating your old, boring pizza cold turkey.

Do yourself a favor.

Come to *Ginanelli's Pizza* with an
open mind and an appetite.

We guarantee you'll be a lifetime fan of *Ginanelli's* with your first bite!

Main Idea and Details

1. What is the main idea of this ad?

    a. Some pizza is boring.

    b. Ginanelli's serves the best pizza.

    c. Pizza is healthy food.

2. What does Ginanelli's Pizza serve besides pizza?

    a. turkey

    b. salad

    c. neither of the above

3. What is special about the crust of Ginanelli's pizza?

    a. It is deep-dish.

    b. It is soft.

    c. It is shaped by hand.

Vocabulary and Semantics

4. What does **bland** mean?

    a. mild

    b. creamy

    c. sweet

5. Which word doesn't mean the same as **pizazz**?

    a. zest

    b. intelligence

    c. excitement

6. Which word is a synonym for **exotic**?

    a. unusual

    b. ordinary

    c. expensive

Figurative Language

7. Which expression doesn't mean the same as **knock your socks off**?

    a. injure you

    b. amaze you

    c. thrill you

8. What does it mean to **quit something cold turkey**?

    a. to stop eating turkey that is cold

    b. to walk like a turkey that is cold

    c. to stop a habit quickly and for good

9. What does it mean to **have an open mind** about something?

    a. to be willing to change your opinion

    b. to be having brain surgery

    c. neither of the above

10. What does it mean if a sauce **packs a punch**?

    a. It is ready to take anywhere.

    b. It is very spicy.

    c. It is full of chunky vegetables.

Asking Questions

Ask a question about Ginanelli's pizza sauce.

Writing and Discussion Prompt ··································

Ginanelli's Pizza guarantees their pizza. Write or talk about what a restaurant guarantee means for customers.

Story 6

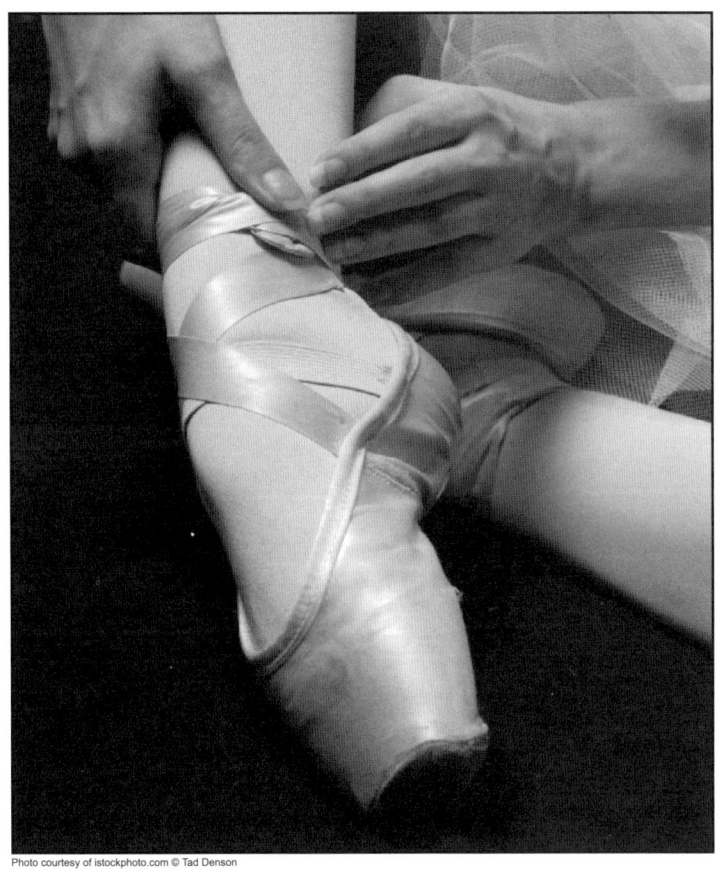

Photo courtesy of istockphoto.com © Tad Denson

Louisa has studied ballet for eleven years. Ballet is her passion and her main activity besides school. Her mother was a ballerina and Louisa wants to follow in her footsteps. She loves dancing for an audience. She has already performed in several ballets at the City Opera House. Today she has been rehearsing for a show that opens in two days.

Things were going like clockwork until Louisa made a fatal leap. As she descended, her ankle turned and she tumbled to the floor. Louisa was between a rock and a hard place. Her ankle was already on fire, but this was her big chance to shine in front of the director of the ballet school she hoped to attend. Only the cream of the crop would be admitted. If she didn't perform and do it well, she would miss her golden opportunity. All her training would be down the drain.

On the flip side, if Louisa damaged her ankle, it might never heal properly. That could jeopardize her whole career. She needed to take stock and develop a plan without delay.

Main Idea and Details

1. What is the main idea of this story?

    a. Louisa loves being a ballet dancer.

    b. Louisa will perform ballet soon.

    c. Louisa hurt her ankle and has a performance soon.

2. Louisa is now sixteen. How old was she when she began to study ballet?

    a. five years old

    b. six years old

    c. seven years old

3. What part of her body did Louisa injure?

    a. her leg

    b. her knee

    c. her ankle

Vocabulary and Semantics

4. What does it mean that Louisa **made a fatal leap**?

    a. She jumped to her death.

    b. Her jump would lead to a problem.

    c. She made a very difficult jump.

5. Which word is a synonym for **jeopardize**?

    a. energize

    b. enlarge

    c. endanger

6. Which word means the same thing as **opportunity**?

    a. chance

    b. career

    c. performance

Figurative Language

7. What does it mean that Louisa **wanted to follow in her mother's footsteps**?

   a. She wanted to learn her mother's dance steps and routines.

   b. She wanted to become a ballerina like her mother.

   c. She wanted to do whatever her mother asked her to do.

8. Which one means the same as being **between a rock and a hard place**?

   a. having a dilemma or a predicament

   b. having two choices of what to do, both of them bad or difficult

   c. being in a tight spot

   d. all of the above

9. Which is another way to say **the cream of the crop**?

   a. the richest

   b. the best

   c. the creamiest

10. What does it mean to **take stock** of something?

   a. to check it out

   b. to take something away from it

   c. to call for help

Asking Questions

Ask a question about ballet and preventing injuries.

Writing and Discussion Prompt ·····························

Write or discuss what you would advise Louisa to do in her situation and why.

Story 7

Alex is absolute poetry in motion on his skateboard. Like greased lightning, he defies gravity and flips in midair. When his feet leave his board, the board magically reconnects like a well-trained yo-yo.

Alex was a natural-born skater from the beginning. He acquired his first skateboard on his sixth birthday. Almost instantly, he turned that board into a magic carpet. His dad bent over backward to help Alex find good places to develop and practice and learn new tricks. Soon Alex was catching air with the best of the skaters practically twice his age.

Photo courtesy of istockphoto.com © Daniel Brunner

It wasn't all a piece of cake for Alex, though. He broke his arm once and had several leg and ankle injuries. Nevertheless, Alex never threw in the towel. He challenged himself to do even trickier moves. "You're a glutton for punishment," his mom said, but Alex knew she was proud of him. His parents insisted that he wear protective gear whenever he skated, and that made sense to him. He wasn't about to risk losing his favorite hobby.

Alex aced the city contest last week. If he sticks to his guns, he'll be the state champion this year.

Readability 5.9
Copyright © 2007 LinguiSystems, Inc.

Main Idea and Details

1. What is the main idea of this story?

   a. Alex wants to learn to ride his skateboard.

   b. Alex likes to skateboard.

   c. Alex is an expert skateboard rider.

2. What kind of injuries has Alex had from skateboarding?

   a. leg, knee, and arm injuries

   b. leg, ankle, and arm injuries

   c. head, leg, and arm injuries

3. How does Alex try to prevent getting injured on his skateboard?

   a. He wears equipment to protect his body.

   b. He only skates when a trainer can guard him.

   c. both *a* and *b*

Vocabulary and Semantics

4. What does it mean to **defy gravity**?

   a. to get angry at gravity

   b. to ignore gravity

   c. to overcome gravity

5. What is a **magic carpet**?

   a. a special rug that helps to train skateboarders

   b. an imaginary rug that flies through the air

   c. a rug that never needs cleaning and can skate

6. **Alex aced the city contest last week**. What does that mean?

   a. He skipped the contest.

   b. He signed up for the contest.

   c. He performed extremely well in the contest.

Figurative Language

7. Which expression doesn't mean the same thing as **bend over backward**?

   a. go the extra mile

   b. bend the rules

   c. do everything possible

8. What does it mean to be **poetry in motion**?

   a. to be emotionally moving

   b. to be beautifully graceful

   c. both *a* and *b*

9. Which statement about Alex is not true?

   a. He was determined to skate even better.

   b. He was reckless about skateboarding.

   c. He had good body coordination.

10. Why did Alex want to stick to his guns?

    a. to be a better shooter

    b. to win the state championship for shooting

    c. so no one would take his guns from him

    d. none of the above

Asking Questions

Ask a question about skateboard safety.

Writing and Discussion Prompt ·······························

Describe the skills or accomplishments of an athlete you admire. Explain why this person has impressed you.

Story 8

Brianna runs like the wind every chance she gets. She races like a well-oiled machine with great endurance. Her running is not what makes her so special, though. She is no run-of-the-mill girl by any stretch of the imagination.

Brianna lost her sight at birth due to medical complications. Her parents were determined to give her every opportunity to function normally, even without sight. Brianna received special education services from her infancy. She exceeded everyone's expectations from the get-go. She walked and talked as early as most babies. In school, she learned to read and write in Braille. She also took tap dance lessons.

Since her dad coached track, it came as no surprise that Brianna liked to run. Her dad engineered a special railing around a track so Brianna could get the feel of track racing. By the time she was in second grade, she was in races with students who had normal sight.

Eventually, Brianna learned to run on different kinds of surfaces. Her favorite place to run now is a nearby dirt road. This road is off-limits to vehicles, so it is an ideal place to run. Brianna always runs with a sighted partner for safety. The partner usually has to put the pedal to the metal to keep up with her.

Main Idea and Details

1. What is the main idea of this story?

   a. Brianna is special.

   b. Brianna is blind.

   c. Brianna loves to run.

2. What job did Brianna's dad have?

   a. football coach

   b. baseball coach

   c. track coach

3. What method did Brianna use to read and write?

   a. Braille

   b. Apple

   c. IBM PC

Vocabulary and Semantics

4. Which word is a synonym for **endurance**?

   a. hardship

   b. stamina

   c. courage

5. Which word does not mean the same as **run-of-the-mill**?

   a. average

   b. unique

   c. ordinary

6. Which is not a meaning for **exceed**?

   a. surpass

   b. go beyond

   c. replace

Figurative Language

7. What does it mean to **run like a well-oiled machine**?

   a. to run smoothly at a steady pace

   b. to run quietly

   c. to run with great force or power

8. What does it mean to **put the pedal to the metal** while you are running?

   a. to wear protective equipment for safety

   b. to stop suddenly

   c. to start running as fast as you can

9. What does **by any stretch of the imagination** mean?

   a. in any way you could think about something

   b. by having a nightmare

   c. by pretending or wishing something would be true

Asking Questions

Ask a question about Brianna learning to tap-dance.

Writing and Discussion Prompt ·······························

Explain how your life would change if you suddenly lost your sight for some reason. Would you find ways to enjoy some of the things you enjoy doing now? How would you spend your free time? What career might you choose for your future?

Story 9

Kelsey, a baseball fanatic, is the only girl in a family with four older siblings. All of her brothers play on baseball teams, and her oldest brother is already a minor league pitcher. It's no wonder Kelsey is addicted to baseball; she was practically born with a glove on her hand. She was raised on baseball lore and never lacked coaching or a partner to play ball.

Photo courtesy of istockphoto.com © Sean Locke

Kelsey now plays fast-pitch softball for her high school team. She's a crackerjack pitcher with a mean curveball and a deceptive riseball. She also plays outfield positions well, rarely missing a catch. Runners need to think twice before trying to steal a base when Kelsey's in the field. She's deadly!

Beyond being a skillful player, Kelsey simply enjoys the sport. She is also a "can-do" organizer who easily gets the ball rolling for any project she tackles. Whenever there's a gathering of friends or family, Kelsey gets a game going pronto.

This summer, Kelsey started a day camp for girls in grades two to four. She teaches them softball fundamentals and also sportsmanship. "Playing ball is great training for life," Kelsey observed. "Your whole team does better when each player pays attention and pulls his weight. Sometimes you win, sometimes you lose. No matter what happens, you play your best and support your team."

Main Idea and Details

1. What is the main idea of this story?

    a. Girls can play baseball as well as boys.

    b. Kelsey enjoys playing baseball.

    c. Kelsey will start a day camp for baseball.

2. How many of Kelsey's brothers are younger than she is?

    a. two

    b. one

    c. none

3. Girls in grades _____ can enroll in Kelsey's day camp.

    a. one to three

    b. two to four

    c. four to six

Vocabulary and Semantics

4. What is a **baseball fanatic**?

    a. someone who really enjoys baseball

    b. someone who only likes baseball

    c. someone who is related to a professional baseball player

5. What is a **sibling**?

    a. a cousin

    b. a very good friend

    c. a brother or sister

6. Which word does not mean the same as **pronto**?

    a. later

    b. immediately

    c. promptly

Figurative Language

7. What is a **crackerjack pitcher**?

   a. a pitcher who eats Cracker Jacks

   b. an exceptionally good pitcher

   c. someone who is learning how to pitch

8. **Kelsey was practically born with a glove on her hand**. What does that mean?

   a. She was polite and wore gloves even when she was little.

   b. She wore gloves almost as soon as she was born.

   c. She was exposed to baseball from her youngest days.

9. What does it mean to **get the ball rolling**?

   a. to throw the first pitch in a baseball game

   b. to start something

   c. to be the first to score a home run in a game

10. What does it mean that **Kelsey is deadly** when it comes to a runner trying to steal a base?

   a. She will kill a runner who tries to steal a base.

   b. She will argue with a runner who tries to steal a base.

   c. She will throw a ball fast enough to the base player to tag the runner out.

Asking Questions

Ask a question about having a career in baseball.

Writing and Discussion Prompt ••••••••••••••••••••••••••••••

Kelsey was lucky to share her enthusiasm for baseball with her brothers. If you could have four siblings who enjoyed something you like, what would you choose to enjoy together? Why?

Story 10

Photo courtesy of istockphoto.com © Roberta Osborne

One reason Naomi considers herself incredibly lucky is that her grandma, Isabella Ricardo, lives with Naomi's family. That makes it easy to spend time together. For as long as Naomi can remember, her grandma has been her rock. Her grandma read to her and talked with her as a child, often telling stories of her own youth. When Naomi's mom died, her grandma stepped up to the plate. She pitched in to raise Naomi and her three siblings.

People say that Naomi and her grandma are peas in a pod. They enjoy the same activities, especially cooking. By late afternoon, savory scents waft from their kitchen, promising a tasty evening meal.

Naomi enjoys being under her grandma's wing. Her grandma, fit as a fiddle at age 83, may be no spring chicken, but she's as sharp as a tack. She shares pearls of wisdom gathered over her lifetime. She is a model of patience and has learned not to be judgmental. She sees the good in people and tolerates the mistakes everyone makes along life's way.

If Naomi's wish comes true, she will someday have the opportunity to fill her grandma's shoes. That's no small goal!

Readability 6.7
Copyright © 2007 LinguiSystems, Inc.

Main Idea and Details

1. What is the main idea of this story?

    a. Naomi admires her grandma.

    b. Naomi lives with her grandma.

    c. Naomi's grandma works hard.

2. Which activity do Naomi and her grandma enjoy together?

    a. sewing

    b. reading

    c. cooking

3. How old is Naomi's grandma?

    a. 76

    b. 83

    c. 85

Vocabulary and Semantics

4. What does it mean if someone is **your rock**?

    a. It is hard to get along with the person.

    b. The person is your main support.

    c. You don't trust the person.

5. **Her grandma stepped up to the plate.** What does that mean?

    a. It was her turn to bat.

    b. She went to get plates from the cabinet.

    c. She filled in for Naomi's mom after her death.

6. Which word means the same as **waft**?

    a. drift

    b. float

    c. both *a* and *b*

Figurative Language

7. What does it mean for people to be **peas in a pod**?

    a. They stick close together.

    b. They are very similar.

    c. They get excited easily.

8. What does it mean to be **under someone's wing**?

    a. to be directed and protected by the person

    b. to hide behind the person

    c. to enjoy traveling together, especially by plane

9. What are **pearls of wisdom**?

    a. pearls from an oyster farm

    b. valuable bits of advice

    c. old sayings

10. What does it mean to **fill someone's shoes**?

    a. to do the same thing the other person did

    b. to find shoes that fit the other person

    c. to put something into the other person's shoes

Asking Questions

Ask a question about being raised by a grandparent.

Writing and Discussion Prompt ································

Naomi wants to be like her grandma someday. Explain who you want to be like someday and why.

Story 11

Marathons have become popular in many places around the world. In the U.S. alone during 2005, over 314 marathons took place. Marathons are now a fixture of life.

How does a marathon develop? It doesn't happen out of the blue. It takes enormous planning. There are numerous hoops to jump through and hurdles to overcome in order to get a marathon up and running. Long before an inaugural marathon occurs, planners must design a course, find equipment, enlist sponsors and funding, and secure support from the community. They must also promote the event and find runners. Volunteers are also a key part of a good marathon.

An important milestone for a marathon is securing more than 1,000 participants. With so many marathons, planners need to woo potential participants to sign up for their event. Most marathons give runners a free T-shirt. Some marathon planners add spice with special events or prize categories. Others throw in a free dinner or movie tickets. Each race has its own reward, and each course has its own charm.

Planning a marathon is a nightmare, but it is also a labor of love. It is a great way to promote health and the community. It brings together people from all walks of life. The next time you run or walk in a marathon, think about all the hard work needed to plan the event. Remember to thank the dedicated planners and volunteers. They deserve it!

Readability 6.9

Main Idea and Details

1. What is the main idea of this article?

    a. It's a big job to develop a marathon.

    b. Marathon road races are popular.

    c. Many people participate in marathons.

2. Where do marathons take place?

    a. only in the U.S.

    b. in the U.S. and in Europe

    c. around the world

3. What is a major milestone for a new marathon event?

    a. having over 1,000 volunteers

    b. having over 1,000 runners

    c. neither of the above

Vocabulary and Semantics

4. Which one is a synonym for **inaugural**?

    a. dance or ball

    b. major

    c. first or opening

5. Which word is not a synonym for **enlist**?

    a. enact

    b. recruit

    c. enroll

6. **Volunteers are a key part of a good marathon.** What does that mean?

    a. Volunteers play an important role in the success of a marathon.

    b. If a marathon has a lot of volunteers, it's guaranteed to be a success.

    c. Volunteers pass out the keys at a marathon.

Figurative Language

7. What does it mean to become a **fixture of life**?

   a. to become elderly

   b. to become a routine part of life

   c. to become useful or handy

8. What does it mean if something **doesn't happen out of the blue**?

   a. It happens on the ground, not in the air or sky.

   b. It just happens by accident or coincidence.

   c. It won't happen without deliberately enacting a plan.

9. What does it mean that event planners **add spice**?

   a. They make the event more attractive.

   b. They add things to get people excited about the event.

   c. They choose exotic, spicy foods for the menu.

   d. both *a* and *b*

10. What does it mean if **something you work on is a nightmare**?

    a. It keeps you awake at night.

    b. It is a challenge that forces you to think and work hard.

    c. You are scared to even think about it.

Asking Questions

Ask a question about running or volunteering in a marathon.

Writing and Discussion Prompt ••••••••••••••••••••••••••••••

There are many ways for people who don't want to run or walk in a marathon to help make the event successful. Tell how you might like to participate in a local marathon and explain your reasons.

Answer Key

Story 1
1. a
2. b
3. c
4. b
5. c
6. a
7. b
8. a
9. c
10. b

Story 2
1. c
2. b
3. a
4. a
5. b
6. b
7. a
8. b
9. c
10. b

Story 3
1. b
2. a
3. c
4. c
5. a
6. b
7. c
8. b
9. a
10. c

Story 4
1. b
2. a
3. d
4. b
5. a
6. true
7. c
8. a
9. a
10. c

Story 5
1. b
2. c
3. c
4. a
5. b
6. a
7. a
8. c
9. a
10. b

Story 6
1. c
2. a
3. c
4. b
5. c
6. a
7. b
8. d
9. b
10. a

Story 7
1. c
2. b
3. a
4. c
5. b
6. c
7. b
8. c
9. b
10. d

Story 8
1. a
2. c
3. a
4. b
5. b
6. c
7. a
8. c
9. a

Story 9
1. b
2. c
3. b
4. a
5. c
6. a
7. b
8. c
9. b
10. c

Story 10
1. a
2. c
3. b
4. b
5. c
6. c
7. b
8. a
9. b
10. a

Story 11
1. a
2. c
3. b
4. c
5. a
6. a
7. b
8. c
9. d
10. b

23-09-9876543